PRAYERS
AND
MEDITATIONS
FOR
HEALING

A Send Your Spirit Publication

Prayers and Meditations for Healing

Charles Toye

A Send Your Spirit Publication

Distributed by the Send Your Spirit Prayer Ministry
21 Copeland Ave.
Reading, MA 01867

NIHIL OBSTAT:
Rev. Thomas J. McDonnell
Censor Librorum

IMPRIMATUR:
✛ Humberto Cardinal Medeiros
Archbishop of Boston

June 17, 1980

The Nihil Obstat and Imprimatur are official declarations that a book or pamphlet is free of doctrinal or moral error. No implication is contained therein that those who have granted the Nihil Obstat and Imprimatur agree with the contents, opinions or statements expressed.

Library of Congress
Catalog Card Number: 80-82813

ISBN: 0-9619732-0-X

Printed and bound in the United States of America

Contents

Preface

If I thirst, I thirst for love. If I am hungry, my hunger is for the delights that come from love. My appetite can be satisfied only by Jesus Christ. He is the center of life, and from his Sacred Heart, all human and divine love flows. If I submit to his will, he will put me into the mainstream of eternity, and all will be done for me. How well I know this! Yet, this is hard for me to do. Because of what I am, I have a normal inclination toward self-determination and self-satisfaction that separates me from Christ and prevents me from surrendering. The Holy Spirit must do it for me. Only he can transform me into the likeness of Christ and make me pleasing to the Father. Only he can lift me up, and provide me with the grace that I need. Send your Spirit, my Jesus, help me in my hour of need.

It is the object of this book to help you make that call, "Send Your Spirit," and to help you to surrender your will to the Lord, with love, through meditative prayer. By entering into the presence of the Father with humility in love, and by reflecting on the presence of Christ realized through the meditative verses in this book, we pray that a spark of the divine touch will engender a flame in your soul.

St. Paul tells us that faith grows by hearing, and Isaiah says that understanding comes from believing. The concepts of prayer that the Lord gave to me, I now give to you. Read and believe in faith with a longing desire for the love of God, and you will soon discover the fantastic power of the Spirit of the Lord that is within you. Just relax in the arms of the Father, and open up your heart to the Lord! From the themes of the Our Father,

Passion, Heavenly Queen, Blood of Jesus, or any of the numerous poems and related material on prayer, you will find some verses that appeal to you. Use them for reflection and through them the Holy Spirit can work within you.

The Our Father meditations were paraphrased from St. Teresa of Avila's work, "The Way of Perfection." St. Teresa is a Doctor of the Church and is often called, "The Mother of Spirituality." She is a true master of the art of prayer.

Some of the Lord's helpers who influenced me during the preparation of this book were Fr. Réal Bourque, O.M.I., who introduced my family into the charismas of the Church, and whose example of Christ changed the lives of my family and myself, plus Sr. Margaret Catherine Sims, C.S.J. without whose inspiration and help we never would have had a prayer ministry. In addition, this book would not have been written without the encouragement of Fr. Kieran Kavanaugh, O.C.D., who taught my family the ways of Carmelite spirituality, or the instruction of Fr. Anthony Haglof, O.C.D., who showed us the beauty of contemplative prayer.

The Spirit-filled eyes of my good friend Bob Chittenden edited the manuscript with great care. To Pat Concannon who helped me with some sections of this book, and to both Ruby Boyd and Helen Winders who shared some of the typing I owe a debt of thanks for their loving attention.

Last, but certainly not least, I am forever grateful to all those of the Paulist Press who made the publication possible such as Bob Heyer, the editor, with whom I enjoyed working very much.

Beauty brings forth love. When you see the beauty in people as I saw it in those who have helped me, then all of God's love comes forth to assist you in many different ways.

Come pray with us, as we say,

Send Your Spirit,
Lord Jesus,
Send Your Spirit

Introduction

The prayers, meditations, and related material contained in this book are an outgrowth from our family prayer ministry, "Send Your Spirit." This ministry was actually founded by our youngest son, Bob Toye, when he was twenty years old in 1978. My wife, Mary, and I assist Bob in this prayer ministry which is dedicated to praying for long-term physical, emotional, and mental illnesses through the means of a Prayer Clock. People send their prayer requests to us and tell us the time of day that they wish to pray.

They are joined in prayer each day with many others through the Mystical Body of Christ for their own intentions and for the honor and glory of God. In this way, they form a spiritual community that builds up the body of Christ through prayer. The prayer ministry also conducts meditation seminars and devotional hours based on the material in this book.

In 1975, when Bob was 18 years old, he was injured in a motorcycle accident that caused him severe brain damage. He was in a coma for four months, confined to a hospital bed for one year, and spent another year as an outpatient. The doctors never gave Bob much hope of surviving let alone walking, talking or seeing as well as he does today. Although we were a Christian family, Catholic by affiliation, we had not gone to church for over seven years. We had simply drifted away from the mainstream of religious activity and thought. Even though I knew that Bob's survival was due to the many prayers of our dear friends, I could not bring myself to have any faith or hope in prayer, the Church, or God. Why? Because no doctor came forth with any wonder drug to cure him, or any surgeon with skilled hands to mend

1

his wounds, or any nurse with such loving care as to bring him back to health, or priest to "lay" hands on him to heal him. Who had a living faith? It is easy to express sympathy to a friend in need. But where do you find the faith to really heal? Where do you find the hope, and where do you find the desire to heal?

Well, thank God, we found it through the urging of our friend Tom to attend a Life in the Spirit seminar and become charismatic Christians. We started out attending prayer meetings as sort of a "joke," and now we have our own prayer ministry. I don't know what denomination you are, or whether you are a charismatic, or would ever think of becoming one. We are not trying to convert you, or baptize you, or urge you into anything. All we know is prayer. All we can give you is prayer. All we can do is honor God in your name for his glory.

Bob knows what it is to lie in a hospital bed month after month without being able to control a single muscle in his arms, legs, or hands. He knows the struggle of fighting for enough breath to speak, or the effort it takes to raise your head, sit up in bed, get in a wheelchair, use crutches, walk with a walker, and finally, to take a step with canes. He knows what it takes for you to succeed when the rest have given up. When Bob went to college, some people asked him, "How did you get there?" "On faith," he replied "On faith."

Faith is what our family has found: "expecting" faith to know that whatever we ask for shall be granted before we pray to the Father through Jesus in the Holy Spirit according to the will of God. We found faith in the name of Jesus Christ through prayer.

It is the intention of the prayer inspirations in this book to develop in you a deeper personal relationship with our heavenly Father through Jesus Christ in the Holy Spirit, in order to give honor and glory to God, so that you can more fully partake of his divine kingdom here on earth.

These are not idle words, for a commitment to Christ through prayer can change your life and those of your loved ones. You can receive the love and peace of the Lord. *'Ask, and you shall receive; seek, and you shall find; knock, and the door will be open to you'* (Mt 7:7-11).

Many of us might feel that we have been asking and knocking

on the door of the Lord all of our lives and still haven't found true peace and satisfaction. This might appear to be true. For even though we might attend church regularly, live up to the Christian norm, and recite our prayers often, we still might have not made a sincere commitment to Christ by surrendering our wills to the Lord so that his divine providence can be worked through us. Whether you have been a Christian for a long time, or are new to the faith, unless you make a firm commitment to Christ in love and faith, then you may not be paricipating in the full fruits of the kingdom of God the Lord intends for you to have now, here on earth.

By making such a commitment to Christ, your faith becomes a living-dynamic *now* experience that does things for you: it protects your loved ones, it cures the sick, it comforts the needy, it consoles the despondent, it provides the strength to live through the day to day trials. You can become a witness to this faith because it is through the imperfections of man that Jesus raises us up to the Father through the love of the Holy Spirit for the glory of God. All things are done for the glory of God according to God's will. To have God's will be done through you according to his divine plan, you must first surrender your will to him.

Through love you must learn to trust God by placing yourself in Jesus' hands and letting him guide you through the spiritual "gate" and along the "way" of the cross to the Father. Jesus is the Word, and your faith grows in him by hearing and learning about him. You will understand your faith by believing, for unless you believe in Christ, he may not help you, and unless you believe in miracles, they may not happen to you.

The kingdom of God can be fulfilled in you by prayer. Prayer is the key to the treasures of heaven. It opens up to you the fruits of the Holy Spirit such as peace, joy, love, contentment, patience, and fortitude. You have been made a temple of the living God, a dwelling place for the Holy Spirit, and all of heaven is within you, just a prayer away.

St. Paul tells us this and much more, for he says that love is patient. To show our love for God and to grow in his love, we must be patient. We all want instant miracles and remarkable cures, but we must learn to acquire patience, pray in good faith,

3

hold fast to our commitment to Christ; in short, to practice faith, hope, and charity before the divine plan can be worked through us. For the Father loves us so much, that if we could obtain just enough faith to fill one small mustard seed, he would remove all the mountains of troubles that we see before us.

God's love is like the sun: it always shines upon all. It is up to us to come out of the shade to enjoy it. With the help of Christ in the Holy Spirit, we can clear away the shadows of doubt and habits of imperfection that prevent the Light that is within to shine through our eyes with the joy and love of the Lord, so that our faith becomes alive and we give witness of the eternal splendor of our salvation, now and forever.

Although the overwhleming evidence in the New Testament shows how the love of Jesus constantly touched the spirits and bodies of those who had remained faithful in the trust and the hope of God, one must always remember that not all who do his works or cry, "Lord! Lord!" will enter the kingdom of heaven, and neither will all who ask for healings be healed. We are healed, or not healed in accordance with the Lord's wisdom which resolves all events with respect to the divine plan of our salvation for the glory of God. However long and tiresome the struggle of life may appear, we can be confident that the Father will provide sufficent grace to sustain our sufferings until we receive our just reward. It is in this spirit that we pray for the Lord's healing power.

Come to us Jesus!
Love us Jesus!
Send Your Spirit!

How to Meditate

This book is designed to help you obtain the fruits of prayer through simple acts of meditation. By spending a few minutes each day in thoughtful meditation with the Lord, you can develop a love for God and a comforting sense of his presence. For if you desire to seek God, then in time, with patience, he will come to you. Sincere desire through love is the greatest asset you can bring to your prayer.

It may take you a long time to obtain an appointment with the President of the U.S.A. or a private audience with the King of England. But the office of our Lord, the greatest majesty of them all, is always open, just drop in. He is as near to you as your heart, and a part of you as your breath. You can enter his presence, sense his love, and feel his peace.

No matter how foolish you might think your life has been up till now; no matter how base you may picture yourself to be; no matter how degraded you feel; whatever your age, you are still a child of God and have been made worthy to participate in the kingdom of God by virtue of the Holy Spirit who resides in you because of your baptism. This was made possible by the death and resurrection of Jesus Christ, Our Savior, the true Son of God. *Fear not! Desire much! Love a lot!*

The prayers, meditations, and poems in this book have been selected to help induce in you the desire of love and faith in God. When you begin to read the book first picture yourself in the presence of Jesus: walking on a beach with him, in a garden, in your house, or whatever pleasant surrounding you desire. Relax, read and pray, let Jesus teach you, and the Holy Spirit will guide you. When you read, stop and reflect on what you have read. It is a good idea to read the book through at least once. Don't be disturbed if at first you do not understand certain verses, or see how they relate to you, or what you have previously learned, for the Lord will fill your heart with what is best for you.

Meditation is a personal act of communication between you and God. You say a short verse, reflect on its meaning, and then listen for the Word of God to be set in your heart. Reflecting and listening are very important. It is then that the presence of God is realized, and his wisdom revealed to us. Think about what you have read. By spending a few extra minutes to develop your ideas, your thoughts will be able to give greater honor and glory to God. They will carry the power of your prayer. It is through such power and the Spirit that the Good News is preached. It is by the power of the Spirit that you receive faith. It is with the power of the Spirit that Jesus teaches and heals.

Teach us Jesus!
Heal us Jesus!
Send Your Spirit!

Prayer Power Is God's Power

Prayer does work! Because prayer power is God's power. Christ preached the message of salvation to the Jews 2000 years ago with prayer power. He didn't rely on highly sophisticated and elaborate philosophical and theological arguments to convince the Jews of the fantastic merits of the New Covenant. Instead, Jesus reached out to the people with acts of love and kindness, through prayer as exemplified many times in the New Testament. The greater majority of his acts of love were demonstrated by healing. He healed people, not to show he was God since he was going to prove that by rising from the dead, but because to the Jews, salvation meant the saving of the whole man, both body and soul.

Jesus demonstrated the salvation message many times through healing to show that the faith of the Good News is a living faith that does things for you. Many of the healing incidents in the Bible tell of how Jesus prayed first before he performed an act of healing, and if he didn't succeed at first, then he simply prayed again until the person was healed. Christ used God's power through prayer to teach what true faith can accomplish according to the divine plan of the Father. Jesus lived that faith through prayer power. He even sent out his disciples to preach the Good News through prayer power.

Once in a while, just like us, some of the disciples would forget to use prayer power when they should. Instead, they would try to rely on their own natural talents and abilities. For example, consider the apostle St. Paul. He was a man of great physical endurance and well educated in the philosophy and theology of his time, having been taught by the great Jewish leader Gamaliel.

After many years of faithful Christian service to the Lord by preaching, teaching, founding churches, performing miracles, and healing the sick, all in the name of Jesus Christ for the glory of God, his travels took him to the city of Athens in Greece.

It seems that when St. Paul saw the grandeur of the city of Athens and heard the eloquence of the Greek debaters who were there, he became ensnared by the false glory of this world, and he thought that he could accept the challenge of debating them on the merits of Christianity by relying on his own natural talents and cunning. A sense of false pride took hold of this well-seasoned champion of the faith as he launched forth in verbal battle with the Greek philosophers. The results were catastrophic. His rhetoric failed to convince them of anything. They even laughed at him and made fun of him. St. Paul left Athens in bitter disappointment and with despair over his failure. Yet, he had enough humility left in him to ask the Lord for forgiveness so that when he came to the city of Corinth, his next stop, he wouldn't make the same mistake again.

This time, he relied on God's power through prayer as we read in 1 Corinthians 2:1–5, *"Far from relying on any power of my own, I came among you in great fear and trembling. . . ."* He was highly successful in this venture for the faith.

Now, maybe sometimes we behave a little like St. Paul did in Athens, we forget God's power. We get so wrapped up in the glitter and splendor of the world that we try to accomplish everything by ourselves. As a result, our once great ambitions now become our uncontrollable obsessions that cause us unending anxiety, or maybe our once enjoyable habits now become our miserable masters that bring us sorrow and despair, or maybe we tried to regulate our lives according to our own preconceived goals and notions and found the frustration of such an undertaking too great to carry as the world and Satan laugh at us for our dismal failure. It seems that the utter miseries of this world and the complete desperation of our own plight so often reach down to the very depths of our own souls that we want to give up hope and abandon everything.

Sickness, death, and disillusionment keep piling up all around us, even when we try to do what we think is right. In spite of

8

all our good intentions, desires, and acts, it seems at times as if God doesn't want to pay any attention to us. Could it be that maybe there is a little of St. Paul's "pride" left in us that we don't recognize, and it is blocking God's power from becoming effective? Pride in one's own ability is one of the worst kinds of imperfections. It caused the fall of Satan and the death of Adam and Eve. Is it through ignorance that we don't know how to get rid of it? St. Paul tells us that faith grows by hearing and Isaiah says that understanding comes from believing. We cannot understand until we believe, and we cannot believe until we first hear the Good News. Now the Good News is simply this: We can destroy the sin of pride and every other sin no matter how deeply rooted it is, or how ugly, vile, and degrading it has become, while obtaining God's power through prayer, if we first make a commitment to Christ.

We make this commitment by first surrendering our wills to the Lord. We ask God to forgive us and to manage our lives. Now, we don't have to run away to a monastery, convent, or hide in the hills. We do it right where we are, right here and now, whatever our status might be in life. St. Teresa of Avila, that great Doctor of the Church, says that before you can expect God to work his will through you, you must first surrender your will to him. She also explains that the surrendering of your will is one of the most difficult and painful tasks in your life. It is not easy by any means.

As Jesus surrendered his will to the Father in the garden of Gethsemane before he undertook the "way" of the cross, we too must submit our will to the Father. Although it was the first step, the opening scene in the drama of Jesus' passion, crucifixion, death, and resurrection, it was second in greatness only to the last time he surrendered his will to the Father, when he was dying on the cross and commended his soul to the Father. Through the eyes of the world, Christ was a fool to have hung on the cross in mockery of what he was.

After Christ's death, the Father raised him up to his glorious triumph and surrounded him with all the bliss of heaven. What the Father has done for Christ, he will do for us if we just let him. If we surrender to receive, he will surely give. If we let go

9

of our worldly troubles, sorrows, pains, hurts, disappointments, foolish habits and material ambitions, the Father will fill us with the manna of joy, love, peace, tranquility and bliss that adorns his table.

We can truly enjoy the fruits of the Spirit here and now, on this earth, as children of God and rightful heirs to the kingdom of heaven. Heaven is within us, Jesus is here, of this you can be sure—for he is just a breath away.

On Praying

The Bible is a great source from which we can fulfill our spiritual needs. The wisdom in the Scriptures provides comfort and inspiration in times of distress and trial as well as giving norms of conduct to live by. In the Bible, we can find a variety of verses, paragraphs, and stories that can be used to inspire our meditations. We may even combine several such segments to develop a particular theme that we want to reflect on. The following discussion on praying is an example:

How should I prepare for prayer? The foremost purpose of our prayer should be to give honor and glory to God from whom we receive grace for our eternal life. The more we give honor and glory to God, the more grace we receive, and the more perfect we become in the eyes of God. Christ told the young man who asked him what he must do to obtain eternal life, that, if he wanted to be perfect, he should dispose of his possessions and follow him (Mt 19:16–22). In prayer, we are following Jesus, and we are seeking eternal life. It is in prayer that we make a commitment to accept Jesus, and through prayer that the Holy Spirit comes to abide within us. It is only through prayer that we can hope to achieve perfection in all that we do. Not by our own merit, but by the grace of God.

To prepare for prayer then, we must do what Jesus told the young man to do: dispose of our possessions. With respect to prayer, the term "possessions" means anything that is blocking God's grace from coming to us, anything that is standing in the way between us and God. A sinful habit, an imperfection in our charity toward others, an obsession with some act that we wish

11

God to do for our benefit or the good of our loved ones can easily become a hindrance to prayer. In prayer, we can and should make a petition to God, "Whatever you ask in my name will be given to you" (Jn 14:12-14). After that, we must put aside all things and follow him, fix our eyes only on him. We should come to pray and listen to what the Lord has to tell us. We must open ourselves up to him, be ready to accept what he has to offer us and then, with patience, wait for his grace (Mt 5:1-13).

How should I pray? You should pray in truth and in Spirit (Jn 4:23). God is Spirit, and those who worship him must worship in the Spirit. To obtain the Spirit you must keep Jesus' word and pray with love. Then the Spirit of Truth, the Advocate, will be given to you (Jn 14:16). For Jesus promised that both he and the Father would come and reside in him who loves him (Jn 14:23). Anyone who loves Jesus will be loved by the Father and Jesus will love him also and reveal himself to him (Jn 14:23).

How much should I love him? You should love the Lord with all your strength, with all your heart, with all your soul, and with all your mind (Lk 10:27). The only thing God doesn't have in this whole wide world is your free will. The only thing that God wants from you is your love given freely. He has always loved you and wants to love you for all eternity, if you freely consent. Give your free will in love: the love of your entire being. Your love for him must not be passion, unrestricted emotion, or just an intellectual assent. It must be the state of your being composed of your entire self. It is a divine gift that is obtained by desire, benevolently granted by God. It is the longing desire for the love of God that allows us to pray in the Spirit.

God gives us the Spirit who is begotten out of the love of the Father and Son. It is only this love in us that is pleasing to the Father because through it we are transformed into the likeness of Christ. When the Father sees the likeness of Christ in us, then we become especially pleasing to him. It is the divine mission of the Holy Spirit to transform us, to free us from our imperfect inclinations, and to elevate us up to the divine stature of our inheritance which was won through the blood of Jesus. But, we must cooperate, we must surrender ourselves to the Spirit.

Why should I pray? You should pray because all human beings have within themselves an inherent unquenchable thirst that drives them to forever seek love, goodness, beauty, and truth. Jesus said that if any man is thirsty, he should come to him (Jn 7:37) and he shall never be thirsty again (Jn 4:14). Only Jesus can satisfy eternally the desires of human nature. Only he can fully satisfy our hunger. "I am the bread of life" he said (Jn 6:35). Whoever goes to him will never be thirsty or hungry. The world, the flesh, and the devil can never satisfy us for long. Their bread goes stale and their water turns foul. We must seek Jesus, for he is the "way" (Jn 14:6), and the "light" of the world (Jn 8:12).

With what should I pray? You should pray with confidence, "Ask and you shall receive"; with determination, "Seek and you shall find," and with endurance, "Knock and the door will be open to you" (Mt 7:7–11). This is called "expecting" faith. Jesus tells us that the Father knows our needs before we ask, and that he will take care of us. He knows our wants in this life. We are not to despair, lose courage, or surrender to adversity. The Father treasures us and not one hair of our heads will be lost (Lk 21:18). Every prayer is heard. The Lord responds according to his divine plan for our salvation. We may not always like the answer. Yet, we must remember that the Father knows what is eternally best for us. The glory of God is shown through our imperfections when they are raised up to the Father through Jesus Christ in the Spirit for their perfection. The glory of God is always shown through the will of the Father when we are obedient to his plan for our salvation just as the Blessed Mother was when she replied to the angel, "Let it be done to me" (Lk 1:38). The Lord will always give us sufficient grace to sustain us in our trials. We must be patient and persistent as the widow who wanted justice (Lk 18:1–8), and the man who wanted some bread (Lk 11:5–8) until the glory of the Lord shines through us.

Then, in hope do we pray? Yes, in hope do we pray. For St. Paul tells us that love is patient (1 Cor 13:4) and we must endure our trials with complete hope in the Father. One day as Christ was proceeding to a house to cure a little girl, a huge crowd surrounded him so that he could hardly make his way. There was a certain woman who was suffering from a hemorrhage for twelve years and no one was able to cure her (Lk 8:43). She managed to come up behind Jesus and touch his cloak. Instantly she was cured of her illness. Jesus knew immediately that someone had touched him because he felt a sudden rush of power leave his body. He stopped to inquire of the apostles and of the crowd which person had touched him. After some delay, the woman came forth, and then Jesus told her that by her faith she had been healed.

This is the type of faith, hope, and courage that we must have in prayer. For if that woman, who hardly knew Jesus, could be healed simply by the touching of Jesus' garment in faith, how much more can we, who know and love Christ and are with him every day receive from him if we persist? Can we pass by the temptations of the world, the flesh, and the devil to touch him? Can we make our way through the crowd? Can we keep our eyes on him to find our way? Just to be in his presence, just to reach out to him with humility and love, is sufficient for our needs. Come to him, stand in his presence with faith, hope, and love, and pray with your very being!

Baptismal Prayer of Faith

Oh! Lord, I know I hesitate.
Oh, Lord, I do have little faith.
I know you will not deceive.
You will help me to believe.
I promise I will never, ever stop,
I will, I will, always, always knock.
I try and try so hard to seek
Just to have a little peek.
Help me to keep up my strength.
My trust and belief are so faint.
Thank you good Lord of heaven above,
For showering me with thy love.
You are the Truth, the Light, and the Way,
Help me to find a mountain of faith today.

Oh! For such faith that I could claim,
I would give everlasting glory
And praise to thy name.
You are so far and yet so near.
How do you get from there to here?
Show me the narrow way through the gate,
Let me hurry so I won't be late.
Just give me one piece
Of the mustard seed,
Let it be my guardian fleece,
My heavenly feed.
You are my God and have all my love,
Send me Faith and Hope with thy Dove.

Praise the Lord!

Come to Jesus

Oh come to me, my little ones, Oh come to
me now.
I do so much love you, love you and you don't know
how.
By my grace, I lift you up. I lift you to my Father
above.
I bring you joy, I bring you peace, I bring you my
everlasting love.
With open arms I await you to run into my embrace.
To hug you, to console you, to wipe the tears from
your face.
To dress you, to adorn you with my heavenly lace.
Oh, little children come to me, hurry don't be late.
You are here on earth such a precious little time to
gain your heavenly fate.
I love you, I love you beyond your wildest dreams.
Heaven waits before you in peace, tranquility; in
brilliant rays of love it pours forth divine
beams.

Desire of Love

My prayer to heaven I know so well,
    The Spirit of my soul will so tell.
Alone in a space of eternal time,
    With a longing desire of love that is all mine.
To thee I give it; it is all I can give.
    Please take it, and accept it, so I can live.
There is no peace of mind; no comfort I can find.
    Please take it, and accept it, don't be unkind.
Without your blessing your love, I am lost and
    astray.
    I cannot go on in hunger, or thirst not one
    more day.
You know my desires, my thoughts, and
    whatever I say.
    Take my desire, my love, forever I pray.
My soul burns and yearns with this longing
    desire.
    With this one idea and hope, I am all afire.
I look to you dear God in heaven above
    To comfort me with thy love.
Just tell me with one glance of your grace,
    That someday I will look eternally into your
    heavenly face.

There Is One

There is one God,
There is one Father,
There is one Son,
There is one Holy Spirit,
There is one Blessed Virgin,
There is one death and resurrection,
There is one kingdom of God,
There is one everlasting glory,
There is one Love,
There is one heaven,
And all is in One.

I have that One,
In my thought,
In my desire,
In my act of faith,
In my heart is the One
That is everything.

Joy of the Lord

The Joy of the Lord, is with me today.
Ah, the joy of the Lord is within me to stay.
No sorrow, no unrest will ever take it away.
For this gift, in thanks, I will always pray.
In the morning, in the evening; all through the day.
My heart bursts, my spirit rises, as if to say,
"Thank God for this pleasure of life.
I have peace in my soul; I know no strife."

I am amazed and delighted, I cannot believe,
That in all this big world, it is happening to me.
The angels, the saints in the royal court of heaven above
Shower me with blessings and grace from God in love.
Now do with me want you want
and say what you will.
I have no anger or resentment, I have my fill.
My God watches over me with his loving way.
Oh yes! The joy of the Lord is with me today.

Praise Party

Let's have a praise party to sing about the Lord, sing about the Lord, sing about the Lord. Let's have a praise party to sing about the Lord, sing about the Lord, sing about the Lord, and the Lord will soon appear.

Lift up your arms to sing about the Lord, sing about the Lord, sing about the Lord. Lift up your arms to sing about the Lord, sing about the Lord, sing about the Lord, and the Lord will soon be near.

Open up your hearts to sing about the Lord, sing about the Lord, sing about the Lord, Open up your hearts to sing about the Lord, sing about the Lord, sing about the Lord, and the Lord will soon be here.

Let's have a praise party to sing about the Lord, sing about the Lord, sing about the Lord, and the Lord will soon appear.

Do You Want to Follow Jesus?

Do you want to follow Jesus?
Do you want to follow him?
Do you want to follow Jesus?
Do you want victory and win?

Do you know that Jesus loves you?
Do you know that he does care?
Do you feel the power he gives you?
It's so strong and it won't tear.

Do you know the warmth of Jesus?
Do you feel it everywhere?
Do you sense the presence of Jesus?
Do you see his countenance fair?

Do you show the joy of Jesus?
Do you sing his name out loud?
Do you shout the name of Jesus,
To reach him above the cloud?

I will go in search of my Jesus.
I will climb the mountains above.
I will hunger and thirst for my Jesus,
Till I find the One I love.

My God Forever

I have my God forever, not just for a day.
Can't you see what it means to me, when
Jesus comes my way.

He is my strength and my power for which
I always pray.
Don't you know, I want to go, to see him today?

I just love him and love him,
That's all I have to say.
He is my King, my Everything. Oh, Jesus, don't
    delay.

I need you, I need you, my Lord,
Almighty God in heaven above.
Comfort me, let me be safe in the arms of my Love.

No troubles or torments will distress me.
He protects me in each step that I take.
The evil he hates, the good he makes,
Oh Jesus, you are so great.

I raise my arms to adore you,
I open my heart to your grace.
Now I see, for eternity,
The love in your beautiful face.

Who Is My Brother?

Who is my brother?
Whom should I love?
I do not know.
Who is my brother?
If it is you, please tell me so!
Who is my brother?
Where did he go?
Is he in front of me, beside me, or below?

All the people of the world,
Who lived yesterday, today, and tomorrow,
Are they my brothers whom I seek with pain and sorrow?
How can I help them, what can I do?
How do I know what is right and true?

Just seek the Christ and look into his eyes,
And whoever follows him, you will realize,
Does the same and acts like him,
Is gentle, compassionate, and seeks no sin.
He will extend his love and be like kin.

And if you find others who don't act this way,
Be gentle yourself and be careful what you say.
Show them Christ's love, extend his hand,
Heal their wounds, comfort their shame,
Give them the light, they are not to blame,
For it is all part of God's divine plan,
That you will find your brother everywhere
You go in this great land.

Turn Toward Him

Did you ever yearn to be with him
When he walked upon this earth?
Then come, turn the eyes of your soul
Toward him now,
And pray that the Spirit within you gives birth.

Did you ever dream of standing at the foot
Of the cross and looking into his eyes?
Then come, turn the eyes of your soul
Toward him now,
And pray that the evil in you dies.

Did you ever think of comforting him
When he carried his cross?
Then come, turn the eyes of your soul
Toward him now,
And pray, and pray; never mind the cost.

Did you ever long to hear one of his
Sermons that he taught?
Then come, turn the eyes of your soul
Toward him now,
And pray, for only with prayer can it
Now be bought.

Did you say that you wanted to be with
Him when he was alive?
Oh no! You couldn't bear it, you shouldn't
Even try.
For if you cannot pray now with all the
Love and grace he has to give,
Then you never would have made it through
All his trials, torture, and pain.
For those were not the times for timid souls
Like us to live, or with him to even remain.

Sacred Heart

Oh, Sacred Heart of Jesus who loves us so very much,
Who brings comfort and consolation with just one
   gentle touch,
Fill my heart, fill my being with your sweet love,
Inspire me with virtue and fortitude with the fruits
Of the Holy Dove.

It is only you I can come to in my hour of shame and
   pain.
Detach me from this vile world, I want no fame to
   claim.
With one drop of your Precious Blood, You gave me
   my salvation,
Sweet and pure,
You made my faith in your love so strong and sure.

Oh Jesus! Hold me close to your everlasting heart of
   love.
In the morning, in the evening, protect me with all of
   heavens bliss from above.
With every beat of my heart, I feel your presence so
   near.
You will always walk beside me and take away my
   every fear.

Oh, Sacred Heart of Jesus, with love to you, I end this
   day.
To give honor and glory to you forever, I will always
   pray.

Come into the garden of Olives and pray with Jesus! Most of the time that we pray, we either pray for ourselves, or intercede for someone we know, or for one who has asked for our petitions. This is rightly so, for Jesus told us to ask the Father for what we desire, and we never seem to run out of needs. Jesus also prayed for his needs, especially those required to carry out his divine mission. Jesus had disappointments too. Like the night that he was arrested in the garden of Olives. He had gone there with his disciples to pray. The disciples fell asleep, and Jesus had to pray alone. Twice he asked them to stay awake and pray, and twice they failed him. That night was very agonizing for Jesus because it marked the beginning of his Passion which would take him to his death.

In the years 1673 and 1674, Jesus revealed himself to Sister Margaret Mary Alacoque and told her of the tremendous love he has for mankind and of the wonderful treasures that await those who return his love. He revealed his heart to her as the source of all divine love. Devotions to the Sacred Heart of Jesus started primarily from these apparitions and initially through Sister Margaret Mary's efforts to proclaim to all what the Lord had revealed to her. On one occasion, he indicated to her that she was to help comfort him for the sorrow he suffered in the garden of Olives when his disciples didn't pray with him, to appease the anger of the heavenly Father, and to pray for the pardon of sinners. He appointed a specific hour for her to accomplish this and to be obedient to what he would then teach her.

In remembrance of this particular request of Jesus, the Church encourages Holy Hours of devotion and prayers of reparation with a view toward consoling the heart of Jesus. The most direct way to God is through the theological virtues of faith, hope, and love. Prayers of reparation in honor of the Sacred Heart for offenses committed against his love are an excellent way of exercising these virtues. If you could enter the garden of Olives for just a few minutes each day, the Lord would fill you with divine consolation and teach you many things as he taught Sister Margaret Mary.

If you come to Jesus without regard for your needs, but with deep love, offering yourself to fulfill his desire for you, then your love will be returned to you with many heavenly favors. The Father knows everything you hope for before you ask for it. The surrendering of yourself for his Son is one of the greatest acts you can do in honor of the Father because it gives back unselfishly to God all the divine love of the Spirit that he has given to you.

To help us understand exactly what happened that sorrowful night in the garden of Olives, we should review the accounts of it as related in the gospels, starting with Matthew 26:36–47. In these verses, Matthew refers to the garden of Olives as Gethsemane which means "olive press." Jesus went with his disciples to the garden of Olives to pray. As he entered the garden, he told most of them to wait for him as he took Peter, John, and James a little further. He stopped again and told these three to wait and watch in prayer as he proceeded to find a spot where he could pray alone. After praying a while, he went back to the spot were he had left the three, and instead of finding them in prayer, he found them asleep. He rebuked them for their laziness and went off again to pray by himself. When he went back a second time he again found them asleep. Once more, he scolded them, for they were not accompanying him in prayer as he desired.

In prayer that night, Christ asked the Father if the coming trials (his Passion) couldn't be avoided, but if not then he would submit to the Father's will. Jesus surrendered himself to the will of the Father according to the divine plan of salvation. Matthew gives an accurate account of the events of that night in a straightforward narrative. The Gospel of Mark gives an almost identical narration.

Luke's gospel, 22:39–47, provides us with a little more insight into the events that took place while Jesus was praying that night. Luke says that Christ made his way to the Mount of Olives, as usual. This seems to indicate that Jesus went there quite often to pray. Luke reveals that as Christ was praying an angel appeared to him to give him strength. Jesus prayed so earnestly that his sweat fell to the ground like great drops of blood.

The Lord can use any of our faculties to communicate with us either directly, or indirectly. His presence can be reflected in the moments of peace, love, and joy that he brings to us. He may even infuse grace directly into our souls so that we sense without knowing how, or obtain a particular state of being without knowing why.

When Christ surrendered his will that night, the Father filled his soul with enough strength from the Holy Spirit to see him through the entire Passion without once losing his inner peace which accompanied the heavenly grace from God. That grace is the most important thing to remember as many of the saints and Doctors of the Church such as St. Teresa of Avila and St. John of the Cross keep telling us in their writings. It is the internal grace we receive from supernatural events, and not any external manifestations that we should be concerned about. This point is brought home in John's gospel, 12:27–36, when Jesus foretells his Passion. John says that as Jesus was praying a voice came from heaven, and the people standing by thought it was thunder or an angel. Jesus told them that the heavenly sign was manifested for their sake, not his.

What did Jesus mean by that? He meant that the real glory in a miracle is shown in the internal grace that it engenders and not in the external signs accompanying it, no matter how wonderful they may appear. It should be the same way with us. We must first seek the grace and, out of God's love, other things will be given to us according to the divine plan for our salvation.

Let us enter the garden of Olives for a few minutes each day to be with Jesus. The only thing we need to take with us is love. The love we show when we turn the spiritual eyes of our soul toward him. Always center on him, always fix your attention on him, always rest in his presence with your whole being, give all of your love to him. You can have faith in Jesus and hope in the Father that the Lord will teach you as he taught Sister Margaret Mary when you surrender yourself to his care completely, without reservation.

This is easy to do. Just close your eyes, take a deep breath, and relax in the love of the Lord. Say nothing, just be there in love! The Lord cannot teach you if you talk. We have two ears and only one mouth. We should do twice as much listening as we do talking. Listening is most important! It may take time and practice, but it is the best part of prayer because it confirms our hope, puts our faith to work, and shows our love of God. Try this for a few minutes each day, and soon you will discover that you don't have to go into the garden at all. The eyes of your soul will automatically turn toward Christ as soon as you close them. The love that you give to him will be returned to you a hundredfold, and like Sister Margaret, you will begin to learn the ways of the Lord. All the love of God flows through the Sacred Heart. Be there, just be there to receive it.

Send Your Spirit

Oh, almighty God, creator of heaven and earth and all things, I stand in your presence devoid of all thoughts, with only a longing desire to love you as you are.

With all my love, I strive to give honor and glory to your name.

I offer myself to You as I am with a sincere sorrow for my sins and a great hope for eternity.

Oh Heavenly Father, I ask through the intercession of the Blessed Virgin Mary and all the saints, that in the name of Jesus Christ, you send the Holy Spirit to breathe into me the "living waters" of everlasting life.

Let these "waters" flow through my body and soul touching every vein, muscle, nerve, tissue, bone and memory to cleanse me of all disease and sickness.

Let the gifts and fruits of the Holy Spirit blossom forth in my body, mind, and soul for your glory.

Come Jesus come, and with your gentle hand touch my heart, caress me with your tender embrace, surround me with a protective shield of your love, comfort me, console me, bring me peace of mind, let your love radiate from me; lift me up to the Father for the honor and glory of God.

Send Your Spirit. Send Your Spirit. Holy, Holy, Holy.

Verse 1:
Oh, almighty God, creator of heaven and earth and all things, I stand in your presense devoid of

all thoughts, with only a longing desire to love you as you are.

With all the humility that Jesus has taught us, Almighty God, I humbly enter your presence to pray. Coming before you without any material possession, I rise above every creature and earthly desire to bow before you in reverence and silence. My mind is empty of all thoughts and awaits your divine grace. My entire being is filled with only a longing desire to love you. It is only this loving desire that I take before you. It is only this desire that I dare keep with me in your presence.

I want to love you as you are; not for what you have done for me, and not for your greatness and power. I love you more than life itself, for without you, what is life? I stand before you awaiting your will. Let it be done to me as you wish.

Verse 2:
With all my love, I strive to give honor and glory to your name.

St. Paul says that the greatest gift we can receive from you is love. Your Spirit is love. The love that you give to me I give back to you for the honor and glory of your name. I give to you what is God-like in me. Only that which comes from you can be called "holy." I search within the depth of my being and in every breath of life for divine graces that I can offer up to you for your everlasting glory. By the death and resurrection of Jesus, by the blood of his body and the Spirit of his soul, I have been destined to partake of your glory. It is to honor and glorify you that I pray. It is for this that I live, it is for this that I love, and it is for this that all creation was made.

Besides my love for you, I have nothing, nothing that it worthy to be in your presence, nothing that is fitting for your eyes to behold, nothing that is worthy of the sacrifice of your Son, and nothing that will last through eternity with your glory. All my love I give to you.

Verse 3:

I offer myself to you as I am with a sincere sorrow for my sins and a great hope for eternity.

Almighty God, without your grace I am nothing. I stand before you, a sinner. My sins have separated me from you. They have added to the burden of your Son. They have driven the nails of the cross deeper into his hands and made his blood flow. All the physical and mental pain I now endure, I offer to you for atonement. The greatest pain and suffering is the tremendous anguish I would have to endure if I separated from you. It is this thought of separation that pierces my heart, aches my bones, and tortures my spirit. Do not desert me, my God!

Almighty God, I am your adopted son/daughter and heir to your kingdom. I have great hope for eternal life. Show me mercy, do not abandon me, give me strength to endure my earthly trials. My hope walks with my love toward your everlasting sanctuary.

Verse 4:

Oh, Heavenly Father, I ask through the intercession of the Blessed Virgin Mary and all the saints, that in the name of Jesus Christ, you send the Holy Spirit to breathe into me the "living waters" of everlasting life.

Come Holy Spirit, come breathe into me the living waters of everlasting grace. Through your Holy Spirit, I am born again, called a child of heaven, and made an adopted son of the Father. By your grace my body is made a temple of the living God. By your grace, I am transformed into the likeness of Christ, my brother. It is you who infused into my soul the heavenly gifts of wisdom, understanding, knowledge, and piety.

Verse 5:

Let these waters flow through my body and soul touching every vein, muscle, nerve, tissue, bone, and memory to cleanse me of all disease and sickness.

Who can heal but you, Jesus? Who can love but you, Holy Spirit? Who has compassion but you, Heavenly Father? Let the grace of God rush through my body and soul to cleanse me of all evil and to fill the void with the love of God. Oh God! Fill my cup with thy grace. Pour the warmth and tenderness of the Sacred Heart of Jesus into my breast. Mix my blood with his! Unite my spirit with his!

Verse 6:

Let the gifts and fruits of the Holy Spirit blossom forth in my body, mind, and soul for your glory.

For your glory, Father, for your glory, send me forth pure and clean to give you honor. Let my soul burst with the fruits of the Holy Spirit. Only in this way can I partake of your joy. Oh, what a loving Father who lets me partake of his divine splendor to shine for all eternity in the light of his love. How you love me God! Oh, how you love me! Transform me, Spirit, into a real adopted child of God, so I can truly call Jesus, "Brother." Work the grace of God into every nook and corner of my soul. Teach me wisdom, grant me knowledge, show me prudence, piety, meekness, and cover me with humility. Shower me with the heavenly fragrance of all your healing power.

Verse 7:

Come Jesus come, and with your gentle hand touch my heart, caress me with your tender embrace, surround me with a protective shield of your love, comfort me, console me, bring me peace of mind,

let your love radiate from me; lift me up to the Father for the honor and glory of God.

Loving Jesus, gentle Jesus, I accept your direction. I tread your "way"; I open your "gate"; I take up your cross. Your burden is light because you comfort me, protect me, hold me, carry me; raise me up to our Father. It is you, Jesus, I turn to. It is you, Jesus, who truly loves me. You see me, You know my problems, You weep for my sins, You feel my pain, and my hurt hurts you. Jesus, You have all the power in heaven alone to make the lame walk, the blind see, and the deaf hear. Hear me Jesus, hear me Jesus, shed my burden, heal me, by just one glance of your sweet love.

**Send Your Spirit.
Send Your Spirit.
Holy, Holy, Holy.**

The Our Father

Our Father,
Who art in heaven,
Hallowed be thy name.
Thy kingdom come.
Thy will be done on earth,
As it is in heaven.
Give us this day,
Our daily bread.
Forgive us our trespasses,
As we forgive those,
Who trespass against us.
Lead us not into temptation,
But deliver us from evil. Amen.

The Lord's Prayer was taught to us by Jesus himself. One of the most profitable and comforting ways to read the Scripture is to reflect on the words Jesus gave to us. In them, we will find ideas that are so rich and fulfilling that they forever nourish us. The early Fathers and spiritual writers of the Church taught that the Our Father was not one continuous prayer, but a little library of prayers composed of seven distinct thoughts. Each one of these concepts represented a particular type of petition that we could make to the Father. Although it is a worthwhile practice to repeat the entire prayer each time that we pray, it is sufficient to select the appropriate petition we desire and to pray and meditate on its theme.

Some of the apostles, like St. Peter, had been very devoted Jews before Christ called them to follow him. They were deeply indoctrinated in the Jewish traditional customs and worship. In fact, the first council in the Church was called over the question of whether or not the gentile converts had first to adopt Jewish customs before they could become followers of Christ. It appears that some of the disciples knew how to pray to God before they began to follow Christ since they knew the Jewish customs so very well. Besides that, they watched Jesus perform miracles and even performed some themselves in his name. Consequently, we may be puzzled when we read in Luke 11:2-4, that the disciples asked Jesus to teach them how to pray.

The thoughts that Jesus subsequently taught them to reflect on represent the essence of the message that he had come to proclaim. Namely, that the power of God within us in the form of the Holy Spirit is derived from the love of the Father and the Son. As such, it is so great that it can free us from any bondage the world, the devil, or the flesh might ensnare us in, if we turn toward Christ in faith, love, and hope. If we surrender ourselves to Jesus, he will never fail us.

In the first verse of the Our Father, the key word is "Our." Jesus is our brother and he always prays with us. He will take us to the Father. It is sufficient to reflect on his presence, and let him come and bring us to the Father as we respond to the Lord's call with deep humility and love. We should listen, just listen to Jesus as he pleads our case before the Father. As we love Jesus, he will love us and the Father will love us also. Jesus and the Father will come and abide within us. Then the Holy Spirit will be born within us and the fruits of the Spirit will be revealed to us (Jn 14:21-24).

The second verse of the prayer tells us to honor our Father who is in heaven. The question to ponder is: Where is heaven right now for us here on earth? Jesus told us that the kingdom of God is at hand (Lk 10:9). St. Augustine tells us that he searched for God in many places, but could not find him. Many people have the idea that God is external to them. He is up there somewhere, and we are down here, and after death, we will see him in heaven. They forget that it is by the grace and power of God that our every moment of life is sustained. It is by his ever-present will that we continue to exist. The love and goodness of the Lord must extend into every breath we breathe, every twitch of our muscles, every function of our bodies. He must support us continuously in all of our actions, or else we couldn't operate, and neither could anything else in the world exist or function without

36

his sustaining will. The baptized Christian has another dimension of the grace of God within him. For he has the Holy Spirit, and the fruits of the Spirit are ready to be enkindled within his soul by a simple spark of love. Where the Spirit is, God is, where God is, heaven is, and where heaven is, all the glory and splendor of the eternal kingdom rest. All is within us by the grace of God.

The third verse asks for the kingdom of God to come forth, that is, to be released from within us and to shine forth for the entire world to see. Let our faith come alive, let it do things for us through the will of God. Christ said that you would be able to recognize his followers by the great things they will do in his name as they extend the peace, love, and joy of the Good News to others.

The fourth verse tells us that in order to promote the kingdom of God here on earth according to the will of the Father, in conjunction with the divine plane for our salvation, we must first surrender our will to him. St. Teresa of Avila tells us that the surrendering of our will is one of the most difficult acts we have to perform in this life. Yet, before the Lord can fully work his will through us, we must completely submit ours in obedience to him. We must turn everything over to him, have unswerving faith and trust in his guidance. This includes turning all our troubles, anxieties, and problems over to his care with confidence that everything will be resolved for the good of our salvation. What more can we ask?

The fifth verse reflects on our life, and the presence of Christ eternally with us each day in the Eucharist. The "day" that this verse indicates is not one day out of our life, but represents our entire life span. What is our life span as compared to eternity? It is so infinitesimally small that it is not worthy to be called a "day." If we gauge it from eternity, then what would we want to have for such a short time to guarantee our eternal reward? Jesus, of course! He will protect us. We find him in the Eucharist, the "bread" of this life. We can have him every moment of our life. We can enjoy him for a lifetime here on earth and be united with him for all eternity in heaven. What could possibly be better? This is what we should ask the Father for each day. What a good and loving heavenly Father we have who provides us with such a wonderful gift as Jesus. Pray then, that Jesus will always stay with you every moment of your life! Never let him go!

The sixth verse emphasizes forgiveness. We must forgive those who have offended us. We must exchange love for resentment. Sometimes this is not easy to do because many hurts run deep within us. Yet, on the cross, Christ forgave those who had crucified him. He exchanged love for hate because in spite of his persecutor's obvious boldness and outward awareness of their acts, they were ignorant of the Spirit and didn't comprehend the devastating evil of their crimes. So it is with many people who offend us. They might even boast of their evil deeds, but many times they are really devoid of the Spirit, and we must realize this and show love toward them. Only love can wipe out hate. Unless Christians show love to the world, this will never be accomplished.

In the seventh verse, we seek protection from sin in Jesus, especially those sins that arise out of our own human nature and keep us separated from God. One such sin is pride which inflates our ego and satisfies our selfishness. The antithesis of these spoiled fruits of our degraded nature is humility. It alone can save us. There is no prayer without it, there is no love without it, and there is no eternal reward without humility. It is the basis for our spiritual life. It will be a jewel as our greatest achievement in the crown which we will receive in his presence and wear for eternity.

Verse 1:

Our Father

Oh loving Jesus! you join with us to make yourself a brother of us creatures. You raise us up to the Father; you pray with us for our needs; you stand with us in the presence of the Father to comfort us, console us, and sanctify our pleas. You proclaim that we are children of the Father (Jn 1:12); Sons of God (Rom 8:14), and rightful heirs to the kingdom of heaven being born again in the Spirit (Jn 3:6): the Holy Spirit of God.

It is through the Spirit that we are able to call you, Jesus, our "Beloved Brother." A truer union exists between you and us than any relationship created in blood, because it is of the Spirit. It is of God and deemed by the will of the Father.

Oh Heavenly Father! majestic ruler of heaven and earth! We thank you for your love that allows your precious Son to join with us and to stand before you in prayer, to honor your name, and to give you eternal glory forever.

Come Jesus, come! Help me to pray; stand by my side, and speak to the Father for my sake.

Verse 2:
Who art in heaven

Oh Heavenly Father! Like St. Augustine, I ask: "Where is heaven?" I searched for eternal happiness in many places: in the beauty of creatures, in the power of rank and fortune, in the desire of ambition, in the glory of fame, and I did not find it. Among the goddesses of lust and vice, I squandered my energy and did not find peace or satisfaction. Not until I detached my desires from the goals of this world, did I receive a glimpse of restful tranquility.

Not until I turned inward to seek the Holy Spirit within the depths of my soul, did I understand where God dwells. For the Spirit has made us holy temples of God. The Lord is within us and we should be there with him, He is just a prayer away, a heartbeat, a whisper; and with all our energy, we should recollect our senses to reflect on him in the altar of our hearts where he reigns.

He resides in our soul with his heavenly court: the Blessed Mother and all the saints who pray on our behalf. The Holy Spirit fills us with his grace as Jesus presents us to our Father.

I can speak to you, Father, as your child, in trust, with respect, humility, and confidence. I need only to find a place where we can be alone, and I can gaze upon you residing within me. Oh Lord, cleanse my soul and make it a place worthy of your presence. Give me the strength to prepare myself for your honor. I give

myself to you, come to me, reveal your presence, surround me
with your love, do not forsake me for I place my whole trust
in your mercy.

Verse 3:

Hallowed be thy name.
Thy kingdom come.

The labor of our prayers is rewarded by Christ in the blessings
of the fruits of the Holy Spirit in the kingdom of God. Through
prayer we get to know the Lord, and to know him is to believe
in him, and to believe in him is to understand him, and to understand him is to resolve all things according to his will, and
to resolve all things is truly to partake of the kingdom of God
here on earth, and our faith then becomes a "living" ingredient
in our lives.

Oh Brother Jesus! You ask that we pray for the kingdom
of God to burst forth from within us so that we can receive divine
consolations and heavenly delights by which we can rightfully honor
our Father in heaven. Give us peace through your presence; tranquility by our heavenly thoughts; love by our desires; absorb our
will with your power; calm our senses with your Spirit; capture
our memory and intellect with your grace, and bring us to rest
in your divine splendor.

In heavenly bliss we eagerly await these fruits of the Holy
Spirit. Let us enjoy the manna from heaven, the food from the
Father's table. Let us rejoice in heavenly delights for the honor
and glory of the Lord's name.

Oh Jesus! How you love us to show us a glimpse of our
eternal glory. Detached from the pleasures of the world, we unite.
Take us body and soul Jesus, we surrender to your desires for
the honor and glory of our Father's name.

Verse 4

Thy will be done on earth,
As it is in heaven.

Oh Jesus! That night in the garden of Gethsemane, before your trials, torture, scourging, and death, you surrendered your will to the Father so that his will could be done through you for our salvation. The Father now asks that we surrender our will to him so that his will can be accomplished through us. I am timid, weak, and afraid. Lord Jesus! Hold my hand, help me with faith to submit my will to the Father.

Help me to yield my imperfections, lowly habits, and wordly ambitions entirely unto Almighty God. Help me to seek the sanctuary of his grace. Let the gifts of the Holy Spirit transform me into your image Jesus to make me pleasing to the Father. My will is yours, Almighty God! I accept the eternal plan of salvation that you have designed for me, and by which I will obtain eternal glory.

I commit myself to you Jesus, to the "way" of the cross. I know your burden is light, but help me Jesus, for my nature is weak, my resolution soft, and I need the help of your love and strength. Guide me Jesus with your heavenly light and comfort me by the knowledge of your presence.

Verse 5:

**Give us this day,
Our daily bread.**

Oh Almighty God! The strength I asked for to enable me to surrender my will, you have given to me through your Son, Jesus, my Brother who will remain with me every day. He is my manna from heaven disguised under the appearance of bread and wine, so that a sinner such as I, who is not worthy to see his transfigured face, can gaze upon him with the eyes of my soul in humility, with respect, and a deep love for his many sacrifices on my behalf.

By his precious Blood, we have been redeemed, and by his love for us, he has invoked the Father to let him remain with us as our "daily" sustenance for this "day," our life time here on earth. Let our life time, dear Father, be spent with Jesus in your service, doing your will. Oh God! You have provided us so well with your Son. You let him remain with us always to be with us, encouraging us, showing us the "way" to you.

In the Eucharist, he nourishes us, feeds us, and strengthens us with his divine grace. No task is too big for us, no evil is too great for us to overcome through his love. Hour by hour, day by day, year by year, Jesus grows within us. You, Jesus, who have all the power in heaven and on earth to heal the blind, make the lame walk, and the deaf hear, heal us of our imperfections and free us from our foolish habits. If some were healed by the touch of your cloak, then grant us, who remain with you each day the same loving mercy.

Verse 6:

Forgive us our trespasses,
As we forgive those,
Who trespass against us.

Oh dear Lord! In surrendering my will to you, I have forgiven all those who have offended me in any way. You have pardoned me for all my offenses against you, and I forgave all who have offended me so that I might sincerely do your will, as Jesus has done, with love and kindness toward all. How greatly Jesus wants us to love one another! For having surrendered our wills to the Father, we have given him complete mastery over us, and we cannot do that without a sincere love for him and all of God's children. Oh dear Lord! Pride in my petty worldly honor has often caused bitterness and resentment in my heart toward those who encroached on my worldly stature. The weight of these offenses against me is nothing compared to the weight of my offenses against you, beloved Jesus, upon the cross.

It is not mercy that I must show to any who offend me, but love. For all who insult me, ridicule me, persecute me, or unjustly accuse me, give me something to offer to you, Father, for Jesus' sake in atonement for my sins and grievous offenses.

Oh Jesus! Teach me to love my neighbor as you have loved me.

Verse 7:

Lead us not into temptation,
But deliver us from evil.

Oh Lord! The most devastating temptations are not those of the world and the flesh that can easily be recognized, but the subtle works of the devil that arise from within me to increase my foolish pride and flatter my ego. Let me imitate the humility of Jesus. With the true virtue of humility as a shield and your love as a sword, I can defeat the onslaught of false pride.

Such pride lures me into a sense of deceitful security because I receive delights and consolations from you, or imagine I am more virtuous than I really am, or think that I possess much strength and could never return to my past foolish habits. Jesus, protect me from such pompous throughts about myself.

Amen.

Blood of Jesus

The Blood of Jesus will ever flow
Wherever justice, mercy and love must go.

His Precious Blood he did give
So that in eternity we might live.

With every drop of his blood he shed a tear
That men might be free from sin without any fear.

For this he suffered with nails in each hand,
Hung high on a cross above the land.

And in his side he took a spear
While the earth shook and darkness did appear.

Savior, Son of God, you are the True One!
Forgive me for the evil that I have done.

In your holy blood my soul is bathed.
It becomes pure and clean, and thus is saved.

The Blood of Jesus prayer is a means of reflecting on the Precious Blood of Jesus that flows from his Sacred Heart for our salvation, restoration, sanctification, and the healing of our mental and physical afflictions. As the human heart is a symbol of love, the divine heart of Jesus represents that infinite degree to which love can be had; not later on in heaven, but now, here on this earth by us giving honor and glory to him through acts of love performed in faith.

The Precious Blood that flows from the Sacred Heart is a reminder to us of the love of God, and the price Jesus paid for our salvation. By reflecting on the Precious Blood of Jesus,

44

we virtually taste the wine of our salvation, and are united with him through the Sacred Heart from which the love of the Lord abundantly flows. Mix the blood of Jesus with your blood through devotion to the Sacred Heart, and the fruits of the Holy Spirit shall flow through your veins in "living" waters to give you the peace of Christ, joy of the Lord, and the love of God. He is Lord! He is Lord! He is Lord!

Come stand at the foot of the cross with us and gaze into his Sacred Heart, and you will feast at the Father's table in the kingdom of God. Now! Here and now, just where you are!

Verse 1:
The blood of Jesus will ever flow
Wherever justice, mercy, and love must go.

The blood of Jesus pours forth from the Sacred Heart the warmth of Christ's love upon our souls enkindling a burning desire in our hearts for the sweet embrace of Jesus, his peace, and his consolation. One drop of his Precious Blood causes this burning desire to fill our breasts with a roaring fire that cannot be extinguished.

"Blessed are they who hunger and thirst for justice for they shall be satisfied" (Mt 5:6).

We hunger and thirst for the "living" waters of the Holy Spirit to come and quench our thirst, put out this raging fire of desire, and bring us to justice before the eyes of the Father. Oh for justice! Where do we find it? Working in the Lord's vineyard bringing the fruits of the Holy Spirit to our neighbors, our brothers who are children of God!

Mercy only flows in the blood of Jesus from his Sacred Heart. Only in his blood is strength given to love the rejected, help the oppressed, feed the poor, and comfort the human misery of this world. Only through his Precious Blood can the power of God be demonstrated to those who live in the slavery of sin.

45

**"Blessed are the merciful, for they
shall obtain mercy" (Mt 5:7).**

It is only by the Precious Blood of Jesus we can hope to alleviate the miseries of others, for we are powerless by ourselves; devoid of any strength, wisdom, fortitude, or love. We must turn toward the Sacred Heart from which all the consolations of God come, being first dipped in the blood of Jesus.

**"Amen, I say to you, as long as you did it
for
one of these, the least of my children, you
did it for me" (Mt 25:40).**

Verse 2:
**His Precious Blood he did give,
so that in eternity we might live.**

We live! We live now, here on this earth with the transfigured Christ. By the blood of Jesus, the Son of God was transfigured to sit at the right hand of the Father and to guide us day by day until we are united with God in eternity. By the Precious Blood of Jesus, God showed us how much he loved us, by giving us his only Son to be with us each day, until we can rest with the Father in heaven. To receive the blood of Jesus each day of our lives is the greatest divine gift we could possibly have. The Father loves us, the Son loves us, the Holy Spirit loves us, and we are all united every moment of our lives through the blood of Jesus—the gift of the Sacred Heart, Precious Blood, sweet blood that brings us eternal life.

**"Unless you drink my blood, you shall
not have eternal life" (Jn 8:54).**

Life through the blood of Jesus! Peace through the blood of Jesus! Love through the blood of Jesus! Eternity through the blood of Jesus! And all is ours through the blood of Jesus!

46

Verse 3:

**With every drop of his blood he shed a tear
that men might be free from sin without any
fear.**

Oh! The frustration, pity, cries, and tears that Christ shed because he saw how men were ensnared by the false ideals of this world. How they were trapped by their own laws, rules of obedience, norms of honor, and regulations of piety. By the blood of Jesus, the Holy Spirit rose from the heart of Jesus to free us from the chains of the world, flesh, and devil. The Word came!

"The Truth will set you free" (Jn 8:32).

We are free! We are free! Freed by the Word! Freed by the Precious Blood of Jesus!

We can do nothing without the Spirit of Jesus. Only through him can we break the chains of behavior that enslave us and keep us tied to our lusty, vile, and degrading worldly habits. We cannot rise above the mire of our degradation unless he lifts us up with his gentle hand. The slime of greed, envy, hatred, jealousy, and pride have been washed away from our souls by his blood and our hearts purified by the tears of his compassion.

Verse 4:

**For this he suffered with nails in each
hand,
hung high on a cross above the land.**

For our justice, mercy, love, eternal life, and freedom from sin did Jesus suffer and die. By only one sweet glance of his loving smile, he could have redeemed us. But no! He chose to be scourged and crucified to show us that the path to the Father is stained by his blood poured forth in love from his Sacred Heart. He showed us the "way" and led us through the "gate." Hanging on the cross, he forgave his enemies, and surrendered his will to the Father just before he died.

47

We, too, must forgive and surrender our will to the Father so that his will can be worked through us in accordance with the divine plan. Unless we forgive and surrender, we cannot enter the kingdom or taste the fruit of the Holy Spirit: the peace of Christ, joy of the Lord, and love of God.

Surrender to receive! Surrender to be rewarded! Surrender to be cleansed by the Precious Blood of Jesus! Surrender to live with Jesus, here on this earth, and forever in eternity with the Father!

Verse 5:

And in his side he took a spear
While the earth shook and darkness did appear.

Oh Roman soldier! Like St. Thomas the Apostle, you doubted the Lord and thrust a spear into his side to relieve your frustration. I too, have my doubts; my moments of wonder. Help me, Jesus, to strengthen my faith; help me, Jesus, to believe; help me, Jesus, to cast away all fear and to leap into the loving arms of our Father. At times, I act as doubtful as that Roman soldier who hardly knew you, Jesus; and at other times, I act as doubtful as Thomas the apostle who loved you very much.

Oh Jesus! Sometimes my doubt is as sharp as that soldier's spear, and it pierces into the very marrow of my bones, shakes my soul, and darkens my heart. What little faith I appear to have! Let my faith rise up upon your blood. Let me speak to the Father for you. For as St. Teresa of Avila said, "Who speaks for you, Lord Jesus? Who speaks for you?"

Verse 6:

"Savior, Son of God, you are the True One!
Forgive me for the evil that I have done."

You are Lord; You are Lord,
Heaven knows that you are Lord,

48

Our hearts are lifted high; our voices do cry,
You are Lord; you are Lord.

By your blood, you are Lord,
By your tears, you are Lord.
In your Sacred Heart, I want to see
An image of my soul that shall be.
You are Lord; you are Lord.

You are Lord; you are Lord.
Every creature knows that you are Lord.
Wash away our sins; forgive our foolish
    whims.
You are Lord; you are Lord.
By your blood, precious Jesus, you are Lord!

Verse 7:
In your holy blood my soul is bathed.
It becomes pure and clean, and thus is saved.

By your blood, Jesus, You have cleansed me from every false desire of this world, detached me from the ways of the flesh, and freed me from the temptations of the devil. Thus, am I pure; in this manner, I become acceptable to the Father. I drink your sweet wine, O Sacred Heart! And it has healed me of the evils of sin. I have seen your justice and mercy, Jesus. I now know of your love; and with confidence, I can call you, "Lord"!

Now, I await the divine fruits of your kingdom. I stand ready to be seized by the rapture of your grace and be absorbed into your heavenly splendor where all things are known and where the tranquility that is placed in my heart will reign forever. My longing desire for your love can only be satisfied by a gentle touch of your grace. To St. Paul, Jesus, love is patient—I wait, I wait, I wait, and wait.

Mix your blood with mine and make it flow through your Sacred Heart, loving Jesus. By your blood, I am cleansed; by your blood, I am saved!

49

The Passion

That night in Gethsemane before his trial,
He accepted his mission without a denial.
He surrendered his will as the apostles slept.
He prayed in blood, tears, and wept.
They came to arrest him with clubs in each hand.
He stood tall and erect above this thieving band.

They scorned him, and mocked him, and with
    laughter
They did sing,
"You call yourself God, and a mighty king,
Help yourself now, you fool of a man!"
Not one came forth to defend him, not one from all
That land.

He had cured their sick and helped their lame,
And now, he was to suffer and take their blame.
"I find no wrong in him," Pilate said.
"Scourge him, kill him! we want him dead."

So they beat him, and whipped him, and
Put a crown of thorns on his head.
No food or nourishment was he fed.
For our sins and crimes, he freely bled.

With the cross on his shoulders, he showed us the
    way.
He stumbled and fell three times on the clay.
He bore the sins of the world with each step that
    he took,
As he fulfilled the prophesies in the Old Book.

They nailed him to the cross and erected him high.
They waited and watched to see him die.

His mother looked on with a sigh and a glance,
As his side was ripped open with a soldier's lance.

Amidst thunder and lightning, he gave his soul
To his Father above.
"Forgive them," was his final gesture
And sign of love.
"Oh, Son of mine! You did just fine,"
He heard his Father quietly say,
"You will reign with me in heaven,
On this great day."

Christ was not a poor man, beggar, rich man, or earthly king, but a servant who had come to serve. Jesus was not filled with envy, hatred, pride, or worldly ambition, but was overflowing with love. He was a lover who loved mankind. He told us to serve and love one another. Then, how could such a person be so falsely accused, brutally beaten, scourged, mocked, nailed to a cross and viciously crucified? Why? Because he couldn't condone pride and ambition, and he couldn't compromise with envy, greed, hatred, or any of the attributes that soon become the hideous characteristics of those who labor for the rewards of this world. Christ's Passion was the antithesis of the world's formula for success.

Most certainly, Jesus could have negotiated with the establishment for a comfortable position of esteem in the Jewish hierarchy. However, he didn't come for his own advancement, but to proclaim the truth and to help others. He was creator and created, he was divine and human, he was law and obedience, and he was all truth. There is but one way to our heavenly Father and that is through him. Along this way, Christ offers a peace and joy in love that cannot be duplicated. He claims that his burden is light and his yoke is sweet. Christ is our "Simon," the man who was forced to carry Christ's cross. Jesus helps us out of love. He doesn't weigh us down with troubles. He doesn't bear down on us like the cross bore down on his shoulders. He doesn't cut us to the bone with curses, or the whip, or mock our faults and imperfections as they mocked his divinity. Jesus doesn't judge us as they falsely judged him, or ridicule our ideas as they ridiculed his message. He would never wash his hands of us as Pilate washed his hands of him, or flee in the face of trouble as the apostles fled the night he was arrested. He would never deny us to the Father as Peter denied him to the world. He didn't come just to be with us, but to abide within us, to bring his Spirit of grace into our souls, to lift us up through this world, and to reach down into the abyss of our hearts to bring out the fruits of the kingdom of God for the glory of the Father.

If our hearts do not reflect some of God's glory in this world, then how much can we partake of it in the next world? Christ doesn't want us to withdraw from this world, but to live in it as his Spirit lives within us. It is through us that his light now shines in truth and glory. As we walk his narrow way of the cross, he will guide us and strengthen us as we leave behind the burden of our worldly cares, habits, imperfections, and ambitions that would cause us to falter along our journey.

The resurrected Christ, the transformed Jesus is a reflection of the justice of God. It is he, who in all his glory, now comes to assist us. The risen Christ wants to make us a reflection of the glorious triumph of his Passion.

Verse 1:

That night in Gethsemane before his trial,
He accepted his mission without a denial.
He surrendered his will as the apostles
   slept.
He prayed in blood, tears, and wept.
They came to arrest him with clubs in each
   hand.
He stood tall and erect above this thieving
   band.

You always knew, Jesus of Nazareth, that someday you would have to atone for the vile, degrading, filthy habits of mankind brought about by the evil, lustful, and depraved ambitions of the world, the flesh, and the devil. You knew, Son of the Eternal Father, from all eternity, that you were destined to redeem mankind from the clutches of sin. You knew, God of Light, Savior of the World, King of Kings, and Lord of Hosts, that you would take upon yourself the residue of all the malicious thoughts, words, and deeds of humankind that were committed against heavenly Love.

And now, Jesus, your time had come, as you prayed in the garden of Gethsemane. As you knelt before the Father in deep prayer, the blood of your humanity shed forth from your forehead and the tears of your great compassion flowed from your loving eyes. You surrendered your will to the Father for our salvation. You drank from the bitter chalice of pain and suffering, your own Precious Blood stained and defiled with the mire of human sin.

To accomplish your Father's mission, you performed the supreme act of love by surrendering your will, and with it all the human love that creation has to offer for the honor and glory of God. Teach me good and gentle Jesus, this act of surrendering! Teach me, Lord Jesus, this act of love! Teach me, my Savior, this act of hope! Teach me, my Brother, this act of faith! Let me be by your side in the garden of Gethsemane now. Let me accompany you as the apostles sleep. Let me feel your sorrow. Let me know the true guilt of sin. Let me realize the anguish of your torment. Let me touch the pain of your bleeding heart. Through all this night of life, it is not I who help you, but you who help me. It is only you who can help, you who can aid, and you who can comfort me now and forever.

If I could only be bathed by one drop of your Precious Blood tonight, Holy Savior, my body and soul would be cleansed and purified for your eternal kingdom.

Verse 2:
    They scorned him, and mocked him, and with
        laughter
    They did sing,
    "You call yourself God, and a mighty king,

Help yourself now, you fool of a man!"
Not one came forth to defend him, not one
from all
That land.

They conspired against you, Lord Jesus. They ridiculed you, and lied about you, Almighty God. Their petty minds aligned themselves with the devil to make a mockery out of divine wisdom. Their worldly ambitions and greed prevented them from seeing the truth and light of heavenly knowledge. Their jealousy and pride blinded them to the divine plan for salvation and deprived them of the Spirit of Love.

Not one came forth in your defense; not one came forth to speak for you. Who is there to speak for the Divine One? Who is there to speak for the truth? Who is there to speak for the Word? Who is there to remove the blasphemy from their tongues? Let me be there with you, Lord Jesus, at your trial. Let me be there to learn of the devious ways of the world. Teach me to release my pride and foolish habits and to learn from you the humility of patience. Teach me to give up my slanderous and backbiting habits, replacing them with love for my neighbor.

It was only your great love for men that restrained you from calling on the hosts of heaven to destroy them with fire and pluck the tongues from their mouths. Teach me such love, Lord Jesus, teach me that love infused with the Holy Spirit. Teach me to love Love, and let Love speak through me to the Father. Oh, Spirit of Love, groan within me and raise up the prayers of my heart and soul to the Father. Teach me Lord Jesus! Teach me love!

Verse 3:
He had cured their sick and helped their lame,
And now, he was to suffer and take their blame.
"I find no wrong in him," Pilate said.
"Scourge him, kill him! We want him dead."

Oh, pure Jesus! You are innocent of all the false accusations that they made and the world continues to make against you. Your loving heart showed only mercy to those who beseeched you. You cured the lame, healed the deaf, and made the blind see again, and for this, you are accused. Let me be there with you, Lord Jesus. Cure my afflictions, take away my pain and sorrow; let me be a witness to the faith, and let me forever praise your name to the Father. You, Lord Jesus, the Word, the Light of Creation, desire only the love of men; and toward your love, they only show contempt and scorn as they flee from the Spirit into the vile degrading ways of the world, the flesh, and the devil.

To be your witness, Oh Lord! Let your grace pour forth from me to show others. Your love is the gift of the Spirit that I desire most. Teach me Holy Spirit, teach me as you taught my Brother; teach me humility and the detachment from worldly desires that I need to be a witness for Jesus. Oh yes! Humility, Holy Spirit, teach me humility. Shatter my pride with your fire, burn out every last stain of foolish worldly ambition that separates me from the graces of the Father.

Verse 4:
> **So they beat him, and whipped him,**
> **and**
> **Put a crown of thorns on his head.**
> **No food or nourishment was he fed.**
> **For our sins and crimes, he freely bled.**

Oh Jesus! I need the holy strength of your presence in the divine sacrifice of the Eucharist to sustain me each day. I need your strength to bear the crown of faith you put upon my head.

Melt my hardened heart, and make it understand the joy of repentance and the delights of forgiveness. Be with me in my act of contrition as I come to know my crown of thorns.

Feed me Jesus with your heavenly manna that nourishes the fruits of the Holy Spirit within me. Let me labor in the Father's vineyard with your love. To sit someday at the Father's table with you and partake of the divine feast that the Heavenly Queen has prepared is all that I ask. For at this banquet of bliss, you shall remove my crown of thorns and dress me with the rewards of salvation.

Do not judge me now, my Brother, while I still wear this crown of thorns, for my flesh is weak, my heart is timid, and I still search along the "way" of my salvation for your guiding light. Come to me gently, Lord Jesus, for I hurt with a longing desire for the love that you have to give. Teach me, Holy Spirit, to know the remorse of each thorn in my crown. Teach me, Holy Spirit, to accept the sorrow of my foolish ways and show me the heavenly rewards of a true repentance. St. Paul had a thorn in his flesh. I have many thorns of imperfection that can be removed only by your loving grace.

Verse 5:
With the cross on his shoulders, he
Showed us the way.
He stumbled and fell three times on the clay.
He bore the sins of the world with each
Step that he took,
As he fulfilled the prophesies in the Old Book.

Oh Lord Jesus! The cross that bore down heavily upon you was made from the sins of this world. The splinters that tore your flesh were made from my acts of transgression against your divine wisdom and love. Every sin of mankind came before your eyes and the anguish they caused sapped your strength and you fell helplessly at the feet of the world.

Show me the "way," Lord Jesus, open the "gate," Lord! Catch me as I fall! Lift my cross as Simon lifted yours! Share my burden, Brother of Hope! Give me grace as the Holy Spirit gave it to you! Free me from the traps of my imperfections and lowly habits! Lift these crosses from me!

Lord Jesus, only you have the power in heaven and on earth to heal. Without your mercy, I am lost. Heal me, Jesus, as I walk toward the Father. Lift me up to him for the honor and glory of God. I cannot lift your cross, Jesus, but through your compassion and love, you can lift mine. Walk with me Jesus; let me rest in you along this journey of life.

Verse 6:
They nailed him to the cross and
Erected him high.
They waited and watched to see him die.
His mother looked on with a sigh and a glance
As his side was ripped open with a
Soldier's lance.

With each pounding of the hammers, the nails of human greed, lust, envy, pride, and jealousy drove deeper into your body, Lord Jesus, to drain you of life. These too, deprive me of my life, my eternal life, and destroy the graces of my salvation. They rob me of my heritage and tear at the tranquility of my soul. Let me be there with you, Lord Jesus, as you remove each nail of destruction from my heart and take it with you to the cross.

Oh, Blessed Mother! Look upon me, a child of the Father, as you looked upon Jesus. Sigh for my life as you sighed for his! Comfort me as you comforted him! Be there beside me each day as you were with him! Hold me in your heart as you held him! For your love, I give eternal honor and glory to your name, Mother of Mercy, Heavenly Queen, and Blessed Mother of Mankind.

Oh, Holy Spirit! Spirit of Love, I need you now as I have never needed you before. I need the sweet juices from your heavenly fruit to quench my thirst for the divine kingdom. I need the gift of wisdom to discern the One True Light of my way. Do not leave me in despair, but strengthen my hope in the Father, my faith in Jesus, and my love in the eternal Trinity. There is nowhere to go; no one to turn to in this hour of my trial, only you to fix my eyes on; only you, Comforter, Holy Spirit of Love. Come fill my body and soul with the "living waters" of eternal peace! For this, I wait; for this I pray!

Verse 7:

**Amidst thunder and lightning, he gave his soul
To his Father above.
"Forgive them," was his final gesture
And sign of love.
"Oh, Son of mine! You did just fine,"
He heard his Father quietly say,
"You will reign with me in heaven,
On this great day."**

You are Lord, my Jesus, you are truly Lord, you have risen from the dead, and you are Lord. You surrendered to the will of the Father in the garden of Gethsemane that night when your passion began; and again, as you hung on the cross moments before your death, you made the final commitment of yourself to the will of the Father. Now, you sit at the right hand of the Father adorned in the heavenly bliss of the eternal kingdom and are Master of all the world.

Teach me your "way," Lord Jesus, teach me love, compassion, to be detached from the ambitions of this world. Teach me to surrender to you, the Father, and the Holy Spirit whom I desire to reign within me forever. Come Holy Spirit, fill me with the graces of the Risen Lord, and transform me into the image of my Redeemer! Fill me now, Holy Spirit with the fruits of your love! Let the Word flow through me from the "living waters" of divine nourishment. I am yours, Lord Jesus, I am yours! Touch my heart with your love, purify my soul with your graces, so that I might return your love through the Spirit to our Father. This is my offering, this is my sacrifice, this is my all, and this is your "way" for my salvation!

Heavenly Queen

Oh, Mary! Heavenly Queen,
How we love you.
Oh, Mary! Blessed Virgin,
The Spirit is above you.
Oh, Beautiful Mother! I see in your face,
The joy of heaven, the Spirit's grace.

Oh, Perfect Mother,
You dedicated your life to him.
Oh, Splendid Lady,
Your Jesus freed us from sin.
If you had said, "No!" where was Jesus to go?
There is none so fair in this human race,
Who would have dared to have taken your place.

Your grace, your life, were above reproach; and for
Your glory, we lift our hearts to give a toast.
We ask you, implore you, to intercede for us;
Plead our case before him, Heavenly Queen, you must!

I am poor, I am lonely; with my burden I am bent,
Hold me close, Sweet Mother, give me courage to
     repent.
Wipe my face, take my sorrow, dry my tears;
Comfort me, console me; remove my fears.

I lay my head upon your breast,
With faith and hope, I seek eternal rest.
I know that you love me, Queen of the heavenly host.
It is for your love, the love of your Son,
That I desire the most.

Splendid Lady, Perfect Mother, Queen of Heaven above
     all things,

For eternity, in praise, the heavenly bell loudly rings.
To your love, to your glory, the heavenly choir always
  sings.
The joy of salvation, the peace of Christ, the love of
  God,
Your presence graciously brings.

There is no finer lady this world has ever seen,
Than the one who resides beside Lord Jesus,
Our Blessed Mother; our Heavenly Queen.

We read in the gospel of St. John 2:1–12, that at the wedding feast in Cana when the last of the wine had been drunk, the Blessed Mother turned to her Son, Jesus, for his assistance. Jesus replied by transforming the water that was there into wine. The chief steward was unaware of what Jesus had done, and when the steward had tasted the new wine, he remarked to the bridegroom how clever the bridegroom was to have saved the best wine for last.

Now, we have done something similar (but not miraculous). We have saved the best "spiritual wine," in the form of the Blessed Mother, for last. If for some reason, you have read the previous material in this book and still have not yielded to the Lord, don't despair or give up because the Blessed Mother has long been the surest refuge for those who need mercy and grace the most. No matter what the problem has been, or whatever the reason as to why you haven't made a commitment to Christ up till now, cast your eyes upon your Blessed Mother, and she will greet you with open arms.

It is true that she is the Heavenly Queen, but first and foremost, she is our "spiritual mother" who will always accept us, intercede for us when we need it, and show us mercy in the name of her Son. To her, we are just infants waiting to be caressed by her love, just as she fondled the baby Jesus. Once you cast your lot in her direction, you will never get it back. She will captivate you with love and compassion. Beauty brings forth love, and the beauty of the Blessed Mother's compassion brings forth all the love in the heavens.

Turn to her as a child of God who is lost, and you shall be welcomed home again! Oh Heavenly Queen, Mother of Mercy, accept me now, lead me home again, for I am yours!

Verse 1:

Oh, Mary! Heavenly Queen,
How we love you.
Oh, Mary! Blessed Virgin,
The Spirit is above you.
Oh, Beautiful Mother! I see in your face,
The joy of heaven, the Spirit's grace.

We love you Blessed Mother, Heavenly Queen, because you are a perfect model of spirituality for us. The Holy Spirit always moved through you. You were guided and motivated by the Spirit of God. Help us, Mother of Mercy, to obtain the sanctity of your gracious ways; help us to persevere in our efforts to please your Son, Lord Jesus. The Holy Spirit is in us just as he was in you, Mother of Mercy, but sometimes we falter; we are weak, given to the ways of the world, flesh, and devil.

We need your compassion and love, Mother of Mercy. You love us, each one of us, for we are your children, heirs to the kingdom of God. You are our Holy Mother who guides us with motherly love. We love you as a mother, and we seek your love as your children.

Oh, Holy Spirit, who filled the Blessed Virgin with divine grace, come to us through the intercession of the Heavenly Queen, and fill us with your Spirit of salvation to make us pleasing to Lord Jesus and his Blessed Mother. Have mercy on your children, Holy Mother, and love me as I run into your arms to seek your protection; your spirit, and the grace of God that radiates through you, Beautiful Lady, down into the depths of my soul.

Verse 2:

> Oh, Perfect Mother,
> You dedicated your life to him,
> Oh, Splendid Lady,
> Your Jesus freed us from sin.
> I you had said, "No!" where was Jesus to go?
> There is none so fair in this human race,
> Who would have dared to have taken your place.

Oh, Mary! Perfect Mother, you dedicated your entire life to Jesus. You gave him birth in a stable, empty of any human comforts. In that naked environment you brought forth the greatest joy that creation has ever seen.

You guided him, taught him; and at times, like us, didn't understand him. But, under your gentle will, he grew to accomplish the divine mission that the Father had sent him on. Oh, Splendid Lady! Help us the same way to accept the will of the Father for the honor and glory of God. For this we pray, for this we ask your intercession.

You surrendered your will to God to accomplish all things according to his divine plan and to live your life in union with his eternal wisdom. Teach us how to surrender our wills to God, to turn our lives over to the Father and to walk through the "gate" and along the "way" with Lord Jesus, our Savior.

Oh. Holy Spirit! Lead me, guide me, spare me from the snares of the world with its false traps of pride, lust, and ambition. Heavenly Mother, protect your children, keep me in the company of your Son, never let me out of your sight—not for a day, not for an hour, not for one single moment of my life. As you dedicated your life to Jesus, I dedicate my life to you.

Verse 3:

> Your grace, your life were above reproach; and for
> Your glory, we lift our hearts to give a toast.
> We ask you, implore you, to intercede for us;
> Plead our case before him, Heavenly Queen, you
>   must!

Oh, Heavenly Queen, Mother of Mercy, intercede for us with your Son. Plead our case before him in the heavenly court. We who are so weak, so afraid, so alone, and so ignorant of heavenly wisdom need your loving intercession. Your Son loves you. He will listen to you. Seek what is best for us according to the divine plan of our salvation. Blessed Mother, I know not my Brother, Lord Jesus, as well as you do. Always be there by my side when I pray.

Always be there, Heavenly Mother, with me in the presence of the Father. Be my strength, my courage, and always hold me close to you as you intercede for me. Just a glance, just a smile, just a nod in my favor is all I ask. It will be sufficient for my salvation, to bring me into the kingdom of God, and to everlasting life with you in the joy of heaven.

Sweet Mother, there is nothing to say, but "Love." There is nothing to ask for, but love; and for God's love, ask the Father, in the Spirit, through your Son, Jesus Christ, on my behalf.

Verse 4:
I am poor, I am lonely; with my burden, I am bent,
Hold me close, Sweet Mother, give me courage to repent.
Wipe my face, take my sorrow, dry my tears;
Comfort me, console me, remove my fears.

Oh, Mother of Mercy, as you watched your Son fall three times as he carried his cross to Calvary, I too fall in this life—many, many, times. It seems that I strive and make no progress. I step out only to fall into the evil pits of this world. At times my cross is so heavy it becomes almost unbearable. I become despondent and want to give up in despair.

I am ashamed that you see me each time that I fall and each time I offend him, your Son, Lord Jesus. Where can I hide and bury myself so deep that you cannot find me? What mercy can you have for one such as I who hurts his Brother so?

Mother of Mercy, give me the courage to repent. Take me by the hand and lift me out of my foolish degrading habits. Send the Holy Spirit to shower me with his gifts that I might be "born again" into your spiritual family and nourished by the "living waters" that flow from your intercession. You, Heavenly Queen, who are the refuge for sinners, harbor me in your gentle arms.

Verse 5:

I lay my head upon your breast,
With faith and hope, I seek eternal rest.
I know that you love me, Queen of the Heavenly Host.
It is for your love, the love of your Son,
That I desire the most.

Oh! Queen of the Heavenly Host, it is your love and that of your Son, Lord Jesus that I truly seek. I bring to my prayer that longing desire for the love of God that strives for a perfect act of faith. I place my hope in the Father, and pray that you, Sweet Mother, will never abandon my cause, that you will always be near me. I know that I can rest in you. I know that I can find through your love the peace of Christ, the love of God, and the joy of the Lord.

I am confident of your mercy and love for me. I find assurance in your love. Your presence lifts my spirit. Now I am sure of my place as a child of God, as an heir to the Father's kingdom, and a child of yours, Sweet Mother.

Verse 6:

Splendid Lady, Perfect Mother, Queen of Heaven above
all things
For eternity, in praise, the heavenly bell loudly rings.
To your love, to your glory, the heavenly choir always
sings.
The joy of salvation, the peace of Christ; the love of
God,
Your presence graciously brings.

Oh, Blessed Mother! Your life was a model of humility. You kept everything Jesus did in your dear heart. You watched him

64

grow and were pleased with him as he completed his Heavenly
Father's mission. You patiently stood by him from birth to death,
and happily rejoiced with him when he rose from the dead. Through
all of this, you sought neither fame nor glory, but willingly passed
everything on to him. Teach us to live the same way, Gracious
Mother.

Queen of Heaven, do not let us be bothered by the demands
of this world. Show us how to seek the peace and tranquility
of the Lord, not for our sake, but for the honor and glory of
God.

For the virtuous way of your life, loving mother, the good
Lord lifted you bodily into heaven where you now reign as Queen
of Heaven above the angels, the blessed, and all righteous souls.
And yet, as the rays of bliss shine from your beautiful face and
the hosts of heaven pay everlasting homage to you, with your
simple humility, you still remain my mother, my pure and gentle
mother ready to comfort and console me, to assist me in any
way that you can. Take my hand, hold me close to you, and
never let me go!

Verse 7:
There is no finer lady, that this world has ever seen,
Than the one who resides beside Lord Jesus,
Our Blessed Mother; our Heavenly Queen.

Oh! Heavenly Queen,
Blessed Virgin,
Beautiful Mother,
Perfect Mother,
Splendid Lady,
Sweet Mother,
Mother of Mercy,
What more can I say,
Than, "I love you."
And, it will always
Be that way.

Hail Mary, full of grace!

Heavenly Queen, Mother of our Savior, you are the great intercessor for mankind. Your Son grants his mother's wishes. At the feast of Cana, he turned water into wine when you asked for his help. Now, Blessed Virgin, intercede for me, turn my troubled waters of despair, hopelessness, and abandonment into the wine of everlasting life. Let the "living waters" of the Spirit in the Word burst forth from within me. Prepare for me a place at the Father's table so that I too may enjoy the heavenly feast of the Lord in the kingdom that your Son redeemed for me.

All is possible through your intercession, all is rectified through your love; and all is purified through your grace, Heavenly Queen.

Along the Seashore

As I walk along the seashore on a bright and sunny day, I look across the calm blue water and am amazed at the vastness of the sea. The water stretches to the horizon and far beyond into regions I do not know. It is huge and gigantic, encompassing everything I can see. The water is boundless as is my infinite spirit. The water is the ocean, as my spirit is "I." The water is discernible as waves form from it. Some of the waves are so big and rush ashore with such a frenzy that they disturb and frighten me.

Yet, I know I am safe as long as I do not become engulfed in them. As long as I stay on the shore, they cannot harm me. These waves are like the thoughts of my mind that appear to disrupt my spirit. But my thoughts are not me, my leg is not me, my arm is not me, my ideas are not me, and my knowledge is not me. "I" can become aware of each and every part of them. True, they are part of me, but not me.

I put all my thoughts, both good and bad, in a small corner of my mind where I can watch and guide them until they disappear. I observe them and prevent them from ensnaring my spirit with their troubles and fantasies. As long as I do not . let a thought absorb my entire mind, I can stand back in my spirit and watch it pass. In this way my mind is calmed and my trials end. For I was not created to be entrapped, enslaved, or possessed by any worldly thought, creature, being, or idea.

As I walk along the seashore, the warm rays of the sun shine upon me and reach into all segments of my body. Their energy produces a heat within me that stimulates my very being and penetrates into each breath that I take. The breath that I breathe in contains the same rays that embrace me. It is not "I" that breathes, but the Living Spirit who sustains me. I am completely submerged in the Spirit. He brings me the warmth of his love.

At night, I hear the roar of the ocean, but cannot see the waves. I am guided by the light of the stars and receive the peace and tranquility of my God. When the clouds cover the sky at night, then I walk in faith knowing my Lord is with me. In this darkness, I sense my breath, and I am reassured of the Spirit who is within me. This fills me with joy and comforts me.

The Spirit gives the love, the peace, the joy of Christ to transform me into a child of God to make me pleasing to the Father. For this I was made; for this, I was created; and for this, I give my spirit.

I breathe in the Spirit of Life and through him breathe out the power of God upon all who hear my voice. This is how I comfort, console, and service my neighbor in the grace of my Lord and in the name of Jesus.

I look toward the ocean and close my eyes to calm the waves of my mind. In this darkness, I stand in faith and hope awaiting the love of God—thus I pray; without uttering a word.

As I walk along the seashore, my path of life, everything seems to be in perfect harmony. I see the waves of the ocean and have no fear. I sense the Breath of Life and know my eternal destiny.

Prayer Schedule

It is to your advantage to pray on a regular scheduled basis. The more you can release the Spirit within you in prayer, the more you will actually like praying. Then the love of God will grow stronger in your heart. It is not the words, length of prayer, or time of day that matters in prayer, but the longing desire for the love of God which you bring to your act of faith that really counts.

The most significant ingredient in prayer is this love. If you take anything with you in prayer to meet the Father, then take love, and never leave it behind. In the development of your spiritual life, it is helpful to try to regulate your prayer by establishing a particular time and procedure for each prayer interval. It may not be possible for you always to keep to your schedule, but the more you do, the more you will miss it when you don't. This will develop into a habitual desire that will be a reminder for you to get back on schedule.

The variety of concepts and verses in this book provide an almost infinite combination of prayer themes that you can use for reflection and meditation. However, as a general guide, the following procedure is given:

Monday—Send Your Spirit

The week can start by reflecting on the "Send your Spirit" prayer which is one of basic submittal to God. Remember, it isn't the repetition of verses that is important, but the meditation in love.

Tuesday—Scripture and Poems

Reading Scripture is very important. The Bible is our first choice for inspiration, and no spiritual development can take place for a Christian without it. The "On Praying" section can be used to acquaint you with some parts of the Bible, if that is required. The poems in this book also contain thoughts that can be developed by reflecting on them, and they can be a source of meditative material.

Wednesday—The Passion

The Passion is always a fountain of inspirational ideas. It is a means of bringing us back to the realities of life when we think that our sufferings are unique and unbearable. It is an excellent remedy for self-pity.

Thursday—Scripture and Poems

Scripture should be read as often as possible. The Lord's words are our best source of grace, comfort, and wisdom.

Friday—Sacred Heart

Friday is traditionally the day that belongs to the Sacred Heart. Mass and communion would be appropriate on this day, especially on the First Friday of the month. The Sacred Heart, the blood of Jesus, and even the Passion can be used as meditative material for devotion to the Sacred Heart. Every effort should be made to maintain this devotion each week.

Saturday—Heavenly Queen

Saturday is our Blessed Mother's day. There is no better way to prepare for Sunday Mass than to rest in the arms of the heavenly Queen on Saturday. We should seek her protection every day of our lives.

Sunday—The Our Father

The week begins by our surrendering our will to the Father. As we proceed through the week, we reflect on the Word, are fortified by Jesus's strength, give honor to the Sacred Heart, and are caressed by the Blessed Virgin. Now, we come to be with the Father as children of God. Let us come with humility and respect, out of love, for the delights that we are about to receive are immeasurably beyond our greatest expectations.

Prayer Intentions

Jesus told his followers that whenever two or more of them gathered together in his name, he would be in the midst of them. He also told them that whatever they asked for from the Father in his name would be granted to them. The mission of the *Send Your Spirit Prayer Ministry* is to *ask* and to *pray*: to pray for the sick and for those who need spiritual development, and to promulgate prayer through teaching, writing, and preaching.

An English mystic once wrote that one of the most perfect prayers was the simple word, "Help." If we could but drop to our knees in complete surrender to God and from the depths of our soul cry, "Help," God would certainly hear our plea and come to us. He would lift us up and embrace us with great love and mercy.

But, as St. Teresa of Avila says, this is not easy for us to do. How often have we tried? How often have we failed? We may need help. We do need the advice of a minister or priest, and we need the spiritual support of a loving community. We need to pray that God will help us to surrender our will and to give our problems over to Jesus. For he has all the power in the world to make the lame walk, the blind see, and the deaf hear. As Jesus surrendered his will to the Father in the garden of Gethsemane before he undertook the "way" of the cross, we too must submit our will to the Father.

As Simon had to help Jesus bear his cross, you may need someone to help you carry yours. That someone could be the *Send Your Spirit Prayer Ministry*. We offer ourselves to you, to pray for your intentions: whatever you desire us to pray for. For example, to help you overcome your "St. Paul's pride," to help you obtain prayer power, to help you get God's power, or whatever your physical, mental, or emotional problems may be.

Write us a letter and tell us what you want us to pray for, and the time of day that you will also pray so that we can join with you. When you write to the *Send Your Spirit Prayer Ministry* and tell us the time that you intend to pray, then we put you on our Prayer Clock. In that way, you will be joined together with many other people through the mystical union of Christ to give honor and glory to God from whom all things work together for the good of those who love and hope in the Lord.

We are healed for the honor and glory of God according to his divine plan. Before the Lord can work his will through us to bring forth his kingdom, we must submit our will to him.

The surrendering of our will to God is the same as making a commitment to Christ who will then lead us through the spiritual "gate" and "way" of the cross to the Father. It is easier sometimes to ask someone to pray for us then it is to take a pen in hand and write a commitment to Christ, especially in time of sorrow and despair. But when someone writes to us and makes a commitment in prayer, then one is actually making a commitment to Christ.

The labor of prayer is rewarded by Christ in the blessings of the fruits of the Holy Spirit such as joy, peace, love, and tranquility. For the kingdom of God is just a prayer away.

Through prayer we get to know the Lord, and to know him is to believe in him, and to believe in him is to understand him, and to understand him is to resolve all things according to his will, and to resolve all things, is to truly partake of the kingdom of God here on earth. Our faith then becomes a "living" dynamic ingredient in our lives.

We all want instant miracles and remarkable cures, but St. Paul says that love is patient. To show our love for God, we must be patient, pray in faith, and hold fast to our commitment.

Come pray with us, prayer works! If you have a long-term physical, emotional, spiritual, or mental prayer need and desire to pray in the privacy of your home while joined with us through the mystical body of Christ in a spiritual community devoted to prayer healing, then send us your prayer intentions and the time each day that you will pray so that we can pray with you.

The *Send Your Spirit Prayer Ministry* is a Christian evangelistic organization supported solely by prayer contributions. All Christians are welcome to come, be loved, and to pray with us through Christ.

Maxim and Counsels on Love

The world, the flesh, and the devil are much smarter than you are. You cannot outwit them, so why try? Let Jesus do it for you.

When you pray, stop talking! Listen to him; just be there in love!

The Lord will accept you wherever you are, regardless of your age or condition; just ask him.

Jesus accepts all those who come to him in faith and with hope. He has never turned anyone away.

To pray to God means to stay in love with him.

Jesus never judged those who came to him. He only loved.

The love of God is a divine gift, ask for it!

Jesus heals us for the honor and glory of his Father. It is through our imperfections that the kingdom of God is brought forth from within us. It is through our imperfections that the love of God is shown.

Beauty brings forth love. As you seek the beauty in people you find God's love. He who has little beauty in his life, reflects little of God's love.

God loves us *from* all eternity *for* all eternity, and all we have to do with the time in between is accept his love.

The only thing in this whole wide world God doesn't have is our free will. The only thing God wants of us in this whole wide world is to give to him our free will out of love.

We were created in human love out of divine love to be united with God's love.

Human love is true love when it reflects divine love.

Hate, envy, jealousy, and war exist because we become obsessed with worldly possessions that cause anxiety, fear, and bitterness. If you become obsessed with the love of God, then you obtain everything of value in this world in peace and tranquility.

Take the sustaining grace of God within us and add to it the gifts of the Holy Spirit, and we burst out with the glory of God.

You cannot separate God from the Holy Spirit, Jesus from God, the Blessed Mother from Jesus, nor heaven from the Blessed Mother. When the Spirit is released from within you, you have everything: all eternity, all glory; all love.

It is we who love by degrees. God cannot love you a little, or very much because he has no separate parts or levels of action. He can only love you as God, a love so great that it is far beyond our wildest imagination.